Decadron Diary

Declaup Mary

Decadron Diary

A Family's Journey Through
Hodgkin's Disease

Karen Kondor

To order additional copies of this book, contact:
Xlibris Corporation
1-888-795-4274
www.Xlibris.com
Orders@Xlibris.com
95215

I Won't Let Go

It's like a storm
That cuts a path.
It breaks your will.
It feels like that.

You think you're lost.
But you're not lost
on your own.
You're not alone.

I will stand by you,
I will help you through.
When you've done all you can do,
and you can't cope.
I will dry your eyes,
I will fight your fight,
I will hold you tight,
and I won't let go.

Rascal Flatts

Time does not change us. It just unfolds us.

—Max Frisch

Preface and Acknowledgements

I thought I was ready. After all, it's been seven years. Back then, my kids were seven, five, and five; now they're fourteen, twelve, and twelve. Since then, I held posts such as stay-at-home mom, day care owner, and operations manager for a computer software education company. Since then, the iPhone was created, followed by three more generations. Since then, my house was virtually destroyed by fire and was rebuilt. Since then, good fortune and hard work took me on travels near and far. During a recent trip to the Middle East, I found myself regularly exclaiming to my mom, "Wow, Dad would have enjoyed this," or, "Oooh, Dad would have found this fascinating." Perhaps that should have been a clue.

While Dad was going through treatment for Hodgkin's disease beginning in 2003, I was the family scribe, sending regular e-mails to friends and family keeping them up-to-date on Dad's condition. Several people commented on my ability to write, so I decided to, one day, pen a story of my family's journey through that chunk of time. I planned on waiting a bit so that the sting of the journey wore off, and I would be able to write without collapsing in a heap, much like I did many days when Dad was sick.

So I waited seven years. I didn't often collapse in a heap while writing this memoir, but many days, I was overly emotional about everyday occurrences. And many days, I could be found sobbing in front of my laptop, reliving each day, each moment in time. Apparently, the sting did not wear off as I expected it to. I'm wondering now if it ever will.

That said, I am glad I forged ahead with my intent to create a book for others to read as they go through their journey with cancer—Hodgkin's or otherwise. Maybe it will be used as a teaching tool for physicians, nurses, psychologists, sociologists, psychiatrists—who knows. Or maybe it will just satisfy someone's curiosity. It doesn't matter—as long as it helps.

First and foremost, this book is dedicated to my dad, and the lessons and memories he left as his legacy. But it is also dedicated to my mom and my sister. Through this journey with Dad, we became the Three Musketeers, and we continue to be. I am so very thankful that we all lived in the same city so that none of us had to go through this alone.

I also dedicate this book to my husband, Randy, and our three kids, Rachel, Sarah, and Jake. Randy was nothing but supportive and understanding throughout the journey, and didn't hesitate to step up to the plate whenever I couldn't bear to put one foot in front of the other. And our kids—they were always able to put a smile on my face, no matter how difficult the day played out. And they still do!

I would be remiss if I didn't also acknowledge the support I received from many wonderful friends and extended family members. Helping care for my kids, bringing us meals, checking in by e-mail and phone, and lending an ear and a shoulder as needed helped me and my family cope a little better, without a doubt.

Last, but not least, a heartfelt thank-you goes out to all the medical professionals we crossed paths with over the course of Dad's treatment. Every single nurse, physician, and surgeon we encountered was professional, caring, compassionate, and knowledgeable. We are so very fortunate to live in a city and country stocked with elite medical professionals.

Some names were changed to protect privacy and identity.

Nothing travels faster than light, with the possible
exception of bad news, which follows its own rules.
—Douglas Adams

August 15, 2003: My Dad

Hi, everyone:

I have some bad news to share with you. I know an e-mail seems so impersonal, but we're on our way to Kelowna tomorrow, and I want to get in touch with you before we go. I apologize for not calling you directly.

As some of you may know, my dad had Hodgkin's disease (lymph node cancer) several years ago. In fact, he ended his chemotherapy just before Rachel was born. Rachel just turned seven in May.

Today, my dad was told that his Hodgkin's has come back. He was troubled by fevers, viruses and infections for the last few months, and as a result, went through extensive testing, including two CT scans, lots of blood work, chest x-rays, a bone scan, and a bone marrow biopsy. It was the biopsy that confirmed the diagnosis. It looks like he'll begin treatment next week, with a stem cell transplant sometime in the near future. At this point, we don't know how advanced his disease is, although my dad says the doctors caught it earlier than last time. But who knows, I'm not sure how much you hear after the doctor tells you that your cancer has come back. I have a list of questions that I'll have to ask once we've all had time for this to sink in.

I'll be in touch again when we get back on the twenty-sixth. Hopefully I'll have encouraging news.

Karen

This was the beginning of what would become my e-mail blog to friends and family. Sometimes I sent e-mails daily, other times weekly. It was very therapeutic for me, and a marvelous way to keep in touch with all those who I knew would be wondering what was happening. There were times I felt like I might be invading their e-mail space, but I figured if they didn't want to read it, they could delete it. I received numerous replies to this initial e-mail, offering warm thoughts, prayers, and offers of help.

In the days that followed, Dad was officially diagnosed with stage 4-B Hodgkin's disease. The disease presented itself in his lymph nodes, bone marrow, liver, and lungs. Not good news, especially after a seven-year remission.

With assurances from everyone that all would be fine, off we went on our annual summer vacation to Kelowna, British Columbia, Canada. We met three other families in Kelowna, all with kids about the same age as ours. The moms on the trip were longtime dear friends of mine, and I knew I could rely on them to lend an ear and a shoulder any time I needed it during our vacation. Despite being only one province away, my mind and heart were never far away from my family, and a tear was never far away from my eye.

I met a lot of people in Europe. I even encountered myself.
—James Baldwin

To Mom, Dad and Barb,
August 16, 2003—Hello from Golden!

We found the free Internet room at our hotel! Just came back from supper at the ABC Family Restaurant. The kids shared macaroni and cheese. They were absolutely fantastic in the car! We took our time along the David Thompson and the Icefields Parkway. It was so majestic! Saw a baby black bear eating berries at the side of the road, and also saw the spectacular glaciers. Hard to believe that there's so much ice up there at this time of year. Spent a little more than an hour at the Chateau Lake Louise, just wandering around. *Lots* of people!

Better get upstairs and get the kids ready for bed.

Love you all . . . can't get you out of my mind.

K

I received a newsy reply from Mom, in which she recounted the many times she and Dad volunteered for the Jasper Banff Relay. Their post was at the Crossing–the point where the David Thompson Highway turns onto the Icefields Parkway in Canada's magnificent Rocky Mountains. Dad was an amateur radio buff–his call sign was VE6 JKB, with JKB representing the first initials for Mom, me, and my sister Barb–so he volunteered as a radio operator, communicating between various stations along the relay route. Mom went along to enjoy a weekend in the majestic Rockies with her husband.

Mom also detailed other things that kept them occupied that week–checking my house, spraying dandelions, putting down slug bait, babysitting my nephew, and of course, communicating with Dad's oncologist:

> I phoned Dr. H (Dad saw her last week and she is lovely) today because the whites of his eyes are turning yellow. She says she thinks he has liver involvement and the liver is hemolyzing (breaking down) red blood cells. She didn't seem overly concerned but asked him to stop taking Tylenol during the day so he has suffered for that. He has now taken two and gone to bed to sleep I hope! I took the opportunity to ask lots of questions and she says she is sure it is the Hodgkin's but they need a final pathology in order to treat him properly from the start. I know that is true but Tuesday and the start date cannot come soon enough for us!

Apart from that, Mom reported on all the communication she had with friends and family over the previous twenty-four hours. For many years, Mom was a pediatric oncology nurse, and many of her friends were nurses of some specialty or another. All were very supportive, although terribly concerned–perhaps not the best support in some ways!

Mom is an only child, with her mom, Grandma P, living three hours away in Calgary (Mom's Dad passed away from non-Hodgkin's lymphoma in 1979). Grandma P was anxious to come to Edmonton; however, due to limited mobility, travel was difficult. Mom was spending most of her time at the hospital, and if Grandma P came to stay, Mom knew she would feel torn between being at the hospital with Dad and being at home with Grandma P. I am certain Grandma P's Mother Bear instincts were in full swing, and she was desperate to just give her daughter a hug! In the end, both ladies understood that having Grandma P in Edmonton living with Mom would just put more work on Mom's already full plate. Plus, Dad was, in many ways, a very private person–I hope that Grandma P understood that until he felt better, he needed his space. So Grandma P stayed in Calgary, with Dad's sister, also a Calgarian, staying in daily communication with her (there was no such thing as e-mail, let alone a computer in Grandma P's home; otherwise, she would have received all my e-mail blogs too!).

Dad's mom, Grandma McT, lived in Calgary, as well. I never truly understood the relationship that Dad had with his sister and parents. It was pretty detached, and although sometimes situations like this bring families together, Dad's illness didn't ever mend whatever troubles were already present in their relationship. Dad's dad passed away in 1996, and I remember that relationship being strained too. My aunt and Grandma McT didn't visit Edmonton too often, and that didn't change during this trying time either, mostly because that is what Dad wanted. I know my aunt found it very difficult to be in another city and not have her finger on the pulse of what was happening. She replied to every one of my e-mails, thanking me profusely for staying in touch, and said many times, "I only have one brother . . . he just has to get well!" My heart went out to my aunt and Grandma McT, but I had to respect Dad's wishes. I did the best I could to keep them up-to-date with the goings on in Edmonton—they often got more regular updates than the folks in my e-mail blog did.

Mom's e-mail ended with, "Love and hugs and kisses all round! Mom—and Dad too, you know that! :):):)" Of course, I knew, but despite the smiley faces, I had trouble smiling, and my heart really wasn't in Kelowna.

> Other things may change us, but we start and end with family.
> —Anthony Brandt

August 21, 2003: We're Coming Home

Hi! Just wanted to let you know that we're on our way home. My dad is going downhill rather quickly. They hospitalized him to do the chemo because the risks of infection, hemorrhage, etc., are so great. But if he doesn't have the chemo, he has days to weeks to live. What a choice. I can't bear to be apart from my family any longer, so we're leaving Kelowna today and will drive as far as Golden or Calgary. Will be in Edmonton by Friday. I could never forgive myself if something happened to my dad and I wasn't there.

My mom is pretty distraught. She's always so strong that it's really hard to see her this way. My sister (Barb) is losing it too because not only is she trying to be supportive for my mom and dad, but both her son and husband have been sick as well. I think that Barb is taking some time off work. At this point, I think my mom will be spending most of her time at the hospital with my dad. Despite the critical situation my dad is in, he says he's been feeling better over the last few days, and his voice does sound stronger when I talk to him on the phone, so maybe all of the prayers and thoughts are doing something positive for him!

Depending on how things go over the next week, I may call upon some of you for some play dates with my kids so I can be with my parents. The kids won't be able to see my dad because of the risk of infection. I can't believe how fast all of this is happening.

Anyhow, I better run and get packed so we can be out of here before checkout time.

Chat with you soon,

Karen

It wasn't long before we were on the road back to Edmonton. Not only was I relieved to be getting back to my family, but there were destructive forest fires all over the British Columbia interior, with a major one right in Kelowna on the banks of Okanagan Lake. Air quality wasn't great, and it wasn't so enjoyable sitting on the beach under the hazy glow of the late-August sun with ash falling like snowflakes all around.

During our trip back, we managed to track down sporadic Internet connections, long enough to receive more wonderfully supportive e-mails from friends and family. We also received an e-mail from Mom with a rundown of what was transpiring at the hospital:

> It is late after a long but good day. Dad went down early for a PICC line that was inserted by Dr. H—we've known him for years and wondered if he would want to do this but it went slick as a whistle and now Dad does not have to be poked for blood work, chemo, etc. What a relief! Chemo started at 1:00 PM and also went very well—with a little Ativan, Zofran and Decadron on board he was eating a chocolate bar when Dr. T arrived this afternoon. Barb and I traded place this afternoon, and I got to play with my grandson while she visited with her Dad. Dad went for a walk around the unit tonight and talked with his friend Ian on the phone. He is optimistic and will as ever fight the good fight.

Receiving this confirmed my decision to head home early from our summer vacation.

We arrived home to find that some very thoughtful friends left our fridge stocked with necessities–bread, milk, and juice! I was planning on stopping for these after I spent some time with Dad, but those lovely people negated that extra trip for me. We also found sitting like a beacon on our kitchen table, the gift of a colorful flowering plant that would serve to brighten many dark days.

Back home in Edmonton, AB, Canada, I felt so much better being closer to my family. I spent about an hour at the Cross Cancer Institute with Dad that night, and he looked a million times better than when I last saw him. He wasn't so yellow and drawn, and the circles under his eyes were gone.

He was upbeat and optimistic, and the prednisone was making him eat like a horse! I brought him some juicy Okanagan plums and peaches, and he was absolutely delighted. He revealed to me that, whenever he laid his head back to rest, he visualized the chemo scaring the crap out of the cancer cells, just like an old "Raid" TV commercial (except, to my surprise, he didn't use the word *crap*!). Despite the comforting reunion, I was very cognizant that things would get worse before they got better. But I was also better able to look at the bright side of things, rather than the downside.

Dad was in the hospital for the better part of two weeks. Barb, Mom, and I took turns each day spending time with him. Mom had a horribly difficult time being away from Dad, but Barb and I encouraged her to take part in various activities like attending Symphony Under the Sky, an event she went to annually with friends. We must have driven Dad nuts occasionally, though, because every so often, he declared, "I think visiting hours are for the visitors, not for the patients." And perhaps he wasn't all wrong . . . most of the time, he slept while we were there, but I always went home feeling better for having spent time with him.

Over the course of those two weeks, Mom began eating again and found she was able to sleep a little more every night. Yet she occasionally mentioned she felt as though she was spinning her wheels. I think that, as a nurse, she knew too much, and therefore, analyzed things more than the rest of us did. I always felt a whole lot better when I saw Dad sitting up in bed, eating, with the whites of his eyes white instead of yellow. Mom, on the other hand, looked at the details of the blood work, and listened for the subtleties in the doctors' voices and language that the rest of us didn't hear.

In order to feel a bit connected, and to let Dad know they were thinking about him, my aunt and Grandma McT sent a fruit and cheese basket to Dad's hospital room. On the day the fruit basket was en route, I was visiting Dad, and he asked me to review the information he received about the medication he was on. We noticed that one of the medications had some possible food interactions. He wasn't supposed to eat aged cheese, yogurt, coffee, tea, chocolate, alcohol, and alcohol-reduced beverages for two weeks after receiving the drug. Since his chemo regimen was to come in two-week spurts, we surmised that these things were to be off his food list until the end of his treatment. He very much enjoyed the fruit when it arrived, and other visitors chowed down on the remaining items in the basket—much better than hospital cafeteria food!

We arranged visits with the grandkids during those two weeks, in among various childhood viruses. The grandkids were the light of Dad's life, and he was desperate to see them whenever his blood counts were high enough. Low blood counts left him especially vulnerable to viruses and bacteria, so we had to be very cognizant of the timing of our visits.

During this time, Barb and I attended Dad's Aunt's ninetieth birthday party at the University of Alberta Faculty Club. Mom and Dad were supposed to attend, but because of the circumstances, we attended on their behalf. We expected to be bombarded with all kinds of questions, as many of the attendees were out-of-towners who didn't regularly see Mom and Dad. However, we felt we were up and over things enough to face the questions without crying, and in the end, it did go well. It was a delicious dinner in the company of relatives we hadn't seen in ages, and I was able to stand up in front of everyone and read a tribute Dad wrote for his aunt—again, without crying!

Come the twenty-fourth of August, and after a few good days (the kids and I even went on some outdoor walks with Dad), we heard nurses at the hospital speculating that Dad may be discharged the following day. Dad was quite happy with that prospect as he would be able to sit in *his* chair, eat pizza, watch TV on a less-grainy display, work on his computer, and chat with friends and grandkids without feeling as though he was bothering his roomie. Mom's outlook was slightly less optimistic: "Might as well sit at home and wait for a fever as sit in the hospital [and wait]!" In the end, discharge was not to be, and it was delayed until the twenty-ninth of August.

In the meantime, Barb and I decided to put together a CD for Dad to listen to while he recuperated. Dad had a lifelong love and talent for music. He kept his CD player next to his hospital bed so that when he had trouble sleeping, he could pop in his headphones and let the music lull him to sleep. The CD was composed of songs that his friends and family felt would bring back wonderful memories and provide Dad with a sense of comfort and relaxation. We sent an e-mail to everyone we could think of, asking them to send us the names and artists of a few songs, along with a note explaining why they chose the music.

Mom chose songs that represented the many facets of music that were meaningful to Dad:

"Christmas in the Trenches" by John McDermott because Dad enjoyed pieces that have a story set to music as do so many of John McDermott, Gordon Lightfoot, and Ian Tyson pieces.

"Smugglers Cove," also by John McDermott, reminded Mom of the wonderful time Dad and (my daughter) Sarah had searching for "pirates' treasures" on the Maui beaches in January, 2003.

Dad always enjoyed the fabulous fiddling of "Orange Blossom Special." Dad extended his love of string instruments by joining the Edmonton Cosmopolitan Music Society in the mid-80s. The family cat didn't always appreciate the music Dad produced during his daily practice, but his commitment to learning to play the violin reflected his appreciation for all kinds of fiddle and violin music.

My Aunt's selections came with some wonderful stories attached:

"Donald Where's Your Troosers?" by Andy Stewart. This song was popular when Dad was in grade 12. One day, on a dare from Grandma McT, Dad wore a kilt to school—something that everyone at Aberhart High School in Calgary never forgot, I'm sure! My Aunt wrote, "My brother, Mr. Shy Guy, showing up at school in a kilt! We had them play that song in the cafeteria at noon that day, but he didn't show up—he hid in his classroom!"

"Danny Boy"—Dad taught himself how to play the guitar and became so proficient that he supplemented his university income by playing at "Giuseppe's Pizza" on Whyte Avenue in Edmonton every weekend. One of the first songs Dad sang that Grandpa and Grandma McT loved was this one.

"Canadian Railroad Trilogy" by Gordon Lightfoot—Dad sang it as well as Gord!

"Crying in the Rain" and "Dream" by the Everly Brothers. These may have been the first songs Dad taught himself to play.

Barb's choices reflected her feelings toward Dad, and words that characterized him:

"Pachelbel's Canon": "I chose this song because I know Dad really likes it. I [also] chose it as the song I walked down the aisle to at my wedding because I knew Dad liked it and I wanted him to be 'part of' our wedding." (Dad's first bout with Hodgkin's disease took place in 1995, and Dad made it out of hospital from a blood transfusion just in time to walk Barb down the aisle at her wedding.)

"Fanfare For the Common Man": "I chose this song because I think it is strong and majestic. Dad is admired by many people for his strength, sense of humor, commitment to family, smarts, and willingness to help anyone. Growing up, I thought that all Dad's worked Bingos, worked diving meets, chauffeured their children all over the city, helped them with homework and everything else Dad did. I realize [now] that I was one of the lucky ones."

"If You Could Read My Mind" by Gordon Lightfoot: "Songs by Gordon Lightfoot, John Denver, and Ian Tyson bring back wonderful childhood memories, especially of driving to Calgary. I chose this song because I find it to be a gentle song, and I know that Dad has a kind gentle side to him."

Dad's close friend, and fellow Scot and electronics tinker-er, Ian, put together an eclectic and thoughtful mix of tunes:

"The Skye Boat Song" by John McDermott: "In 1980 our family visited the Isle of Skye and while crossing on the ferry we listened to this song. Oban, the home of [your Dad's] ancestors, is also on the west coast of Scotland and not all that far from Skye."

"Scotland the Brave" by John McDermott: "A good lively tune to remind the 'old guy' of his heritage. Aye, and a mighty fine heritage it is!"

Ian and Dad enjoyed many days of tinkering with PIC microcontrollers. Through their work, they devised some PIC "tunes" that they used playfully in place of things such as alarm functions on valve controllers. The tunes lasted only about thirty seconds, but Ian included them in his list of recordings for Dad—"Jenny Lind Polka," "Morning Has Broken," and "Amazing Grace," to name a few. These certainly produced a surprised chuckle the first time Dad heard them!

We ended up with three CDs full of music, with artists ranging from Roy D. Mercer and Jane Siberry to Bela Fleck and Alison Krause. It took about a month to get it put together, with my brother-in-law doing the artwork for the "album" covers. Dad really appreciated everybody's contributions and listened to the CDs frequently during treatment.

> "When it comes to life, the critical thing is whether you take things for granted, or take them with gratitude.
> —G. K. Chesterton

September 1, 2003:
Eleven Good Days in a Row!

Hello, all!

It's been awhile since I've updated you on how things are going with my dad. As you can see from the subject of my e-mail, we've had eleven good days in a row!

My dad is responding well to his treatment and hasn't had any of the nasty side effects—save for a "funny" tummy two days ago, for which Maxeran did the trick, and some excruciating hip pain last week, which was attributed to his bone marrow working overtime and four doses of morphine barely touched. He was discharged from the hospital on Friday (August 29) and is happy to be at home in his own comfy chair and own comfy bed. He can work on his laptop and watch TV in between snoozes, and although he was extremely impressed with the hospital food (I know . . . he must really be sick!), he's got much more freedom in his meal planning. Due to some of the chemo, most foods now have a metallic taste, so he's experimenting to find out which foods taste the best. So far, tart things like lemonade and cold things like slurpees work for him. One of the drugs keeps him up a lot at night, so he catches up on his rest during the day. He continues with his oral chemo for the next couple of weeks and then begins a new round of IV chemo on the eighteenth of September, which will bring him one step closer to a stem cell transplant. My mom is happy to have him close by twenty-four hours a day as well.

At this point, I'm actually more worried about my mom than I am about my dad. My dad is receiving the very best of medical care, he's responding to treatment better than anyone thought he would, he himself has a good feeling about the outcome of the treatment, and he's got some good visualization going (I think I told you about the Raid analogy in an earlier e-mail). He's been given a fifty-fifty chance of survival, and my sister and I seem to have been able to come around to the point of feeling as though the cup is half full rather than half empty. My mom, on the other hand, can't seem to find the silver lining to this dark cloud. She worries that any of her former oncology colleagues who give her encouraging news are only doing so because they want her to feel better. She worries that when a nursing friend tells her that she's worried about my mom, she's actually saying that she's worried that something drastic is going to happen to my dad. On a daily basis, she has periods of time whereby she feels sheer panic. Although my dad's blood work is showing strong signs that the chemo is working, and although he physically looks and feels better than he did two weeks ago, she continues to concentrate on the fact that a relapse of Hodgkin's disease after eight years is virtually unheard-of, and the fact that it involves bone marrow is not a good sign. Granted, the going will get tougher before it gets easier as the chemo slowly kills off all of the fast-growing cells in my dad's body. She must feel like a Mack Truck has hit her, and she must feel very out of control, knowing that she can't do any more than what she is already doing. Plus, since she lives in the same house as my dad, she has to put up with his ever-changing moods! Nonetheless, she's got a wonderful support network here, and we'll all help her through the psychological phases of grief so that she can reach the Acceptance and Hope phase sooner rather than later.

Again, thank you for all your e-mails and phone calls. Many of you have called and left messages, and I apologize for not returning your calls. Once my kids are settled in school, I hope to have a little more time during the day to return those messages!

I hope all is well with all of you,

Karen

Many of these e-mails were met with stories from friends and family far and wide who knew of Dad's family's resilience. Grandma McT lived well into her nineties, and many other family members survived various diseases and stressors to live long lives. Other replies commented on not letting go of the strong family ties–especially between me, Barb, Mom, and Dad. One of Mom and Dad's lifelong friends, a registered bone marrow donor, officially offered his marrow "at a moment's notice" assuming the blood types matched. And some replies were just plain funny and put smiles on our faces. This reply came from friends who make their home on Maui for several months of the year: "Aloha, Don, please regain your strength so we can see you in sunny climes again," or as the locals would say, "Make good brudda."

You walk past me. I can feel your pain. Time changes everything. One truth always remains the same. You're still you. After all, you're still you.

—Josh Groban

September 15, 2003: Update

Hello, all!

Another quick update for you:

There's really not all that much to tell, and that's a good thing! My dad's blood counts are stable, and he's slowly regaining his strength and stamina. Food isn't tasting as badly as it once did, and he's walking without his cane now. He did have to contend with a bladder infection that hit on a Friday night, prompting a six-hour-long wait in emergency at the U of A Hospital. He tries to stay away from places that have lots of bugs because he is extremely susceptible to viruses and bacteria right now, with his blood counts being so low. Any virus at this point would hit him much harder than it would you and me and could put off his chemo schedule, which we definitely don't want. We need to keep on top of this thing! He will meet with his oncologist this Friday to find out when his next round of chemo begins. We anticipate that it will be next Monday, assuming his blood counts are high enough to allow for it. Once he has that chemo, he'll probably hit an all-time low a few days later, but we'll cross that bridge when we come to it. He's singing and whistling again, which tells us all that he's feeling better.

My mom is also doing much better. She's still a little apprehensive about things, but not so negative all the time. She's taking advantage of this week to spend short periods of time away from my dad *because she knows he's doing well, and once he starts chemo again, it will be awhile before she will be able to do that again.*

So in a nutshell, good news! Thanks again for all of the e-mails, phone calls, and virtual hugs! All the support is extremely helpful, and much appreciated.

Until next time,

Karen

My e-mail blogs became farther apart, mostly because things were status quo for a while. The days were either good or bad, or somewhere in between, but really contained no new news to report. Friends and family continued to check in with us by e-mail or phone; and Mom, Barb, and I continued our team effort in helping Dad rally. We celebrated Thanksgiving at my house—potluck and casual in jeans. Whenever Dad was in the hospital, we took shifts being with him. He mostly slept, and we mostly read books. Mom got some hand quilting done too. After awhile, I got used to seeing him grab the bedpan when he was too weak to walk to the bathroom. Occasionally, as Dad did this, I'd chuckle, remembering my husband tell me about the time he volunteered at a hospital, and brought a patient some ice water in the urinal, mistaking it for the water pitcher!

October 2, 2003: Update

Hi, all!

Just a quick note to let you know that things are going really well with my dad. He's in the middle of his second round of chemo and feels better at this point than he did at the same point in the first round. In fact, he says he feels the best he's felt in months. On Monday, his blood counts were the best they've been yet!

My mom says that she's finally believing that he's going to make it into remission so that we can start the stem cell transplant. The doctors will use his own bone marrow for the transplant, and it involves my dad staying in hospital for several weeks in isolation. At this point, it looks like the transplant process will begin toward the end of October, beginning of November. We hope that he'll be home for Christmas.

Thanks again for all the "checking in" e-mails and phone calls! Your support, whether by phone or e-mail, is unbelievably valuable.

I hope all of you are well. Chat with you soon!

Karen

When a miracle happens, even if not to you, its nature is to naturally expand. You can almost feel the warmth on your face.

—Hugh Elliott

October 24, 2003: Fantastic News!

Hello, all! I'm bursting with excitement!

My dad had a bone marrow biopsy last Friday at the culmination of his chemotherapy, and we finally got the results today. His marrow is free of disease! The plan now is to admit him to hospital on about the third of November to start the whole bone marrow transplant process. The process involves harvesting his own marrow, then giving him high doses of chemotherapy, and then reintroducing his own marrow. It could take up to six weeks to accomplish this, and he may be in the hospital for a good portion of that time. The chemo will put an end to what little hair he has left, and he'll probably end up with lots of sores in his mouth. All that in addition to the normal side effects of chemo.

Nonetheless, we've very successfully crossed one bridge . . . now it's on to another! We hope to have him home for Christmas.

Karen

Can you imagine the smile on my face? Everyone I e-mailed replied that they had one too!

Grief is Newark. It's there. Can't avoid it. The idea is to
hold your nose, hope the traffic's not too bad and get on to
Manhattan as quickly as possible.

—Eli Attie

November 1, 2003: Good News / Bad News

Hello, all! Welcome to my latest installment of "As the Stomach
Turns," starring Don McTavish in the lead role. My dad met with his
oncologist yesterday and received some pretty disappointing news.
As with all transplants, there are a few people ahead of him in line to
get the same type of transplant done, and his transplant may not go
ahead as scheduled. In fact, it may not happen until the New Year,
even though we anticipated that this would all be said and done by
then.

The transplant process is a time-consuming one. As I understand it,
the process goes something like this: three days in hospital for chemo,
home for a week receiving a drug called GCSF that stimulates the
growth of stem cells in the bone marrow, and then five days of visits
to Canadian Blood Services to harvest the stem cells. Then the cells
are frozen while my dad is hospitalized in isolation for high doses
of chemo, and once they're sure they've killed every last cancer cell,
they give him his stem cells back, and he recovers in isolation until his
doctors believe that he's strong enough to go home.

The glitch comes in at the point where he needs to go to Canadian
Blood Services. They only have so many staff who do this procedure,
the procedure takes a full five days, and they can only take one person
at a time. And since there's a holiday in the middle of the week next
week, making only four working days in the week, they aren't doing
any harvesting at all next week. With three or four people in line
ahead of my dad, it could take up to five weeks to get rolling on this
process for him . . . which is a long time to wait when you're in a
brand-new remission. If this is the case, then he may receive another
dose of chemo in the next couple of weeks, just to tide him over until

they can start the transplant process. The downside of that (other than the obvious) is that too much chemo before the transplant process begins can result in not enough bone marrow available to harvest.

The good news is that the CT scan that my dad had done last Wednesday is congruent with what the bone marrow biopsy told us, and that is that he is in remission. All this leads one to ponder the struggle with transplants, given that in order for one person to become healthy again, something bad has to happen to another person. In our case, one of the folks ahead of my dad is awaiting test results, and there is a possibility that those results will not be good enough for him/her to qualify for transplant. Now, although I am desperate for my dad to get this procedure done, I also don't want another family to feel the anguish of not being able to move forward with treatment. I know how I would feel if we were in that position.

So we're in "hurry up and wait" mode again, and my mom and I don't do that so well. On the other hand, my sister and my dad are pretty good at doing that, so I guess that's the other good news!

Karen

Mom and I spent our "hurry up and wait" time fussing. Not that others didn't fuss; the two of us just did a *better* job of it! I, in particular, became extremely un-Canadian and pressured Mom into determining what might be done about reducing the wait. This is when her oncology background was an asset instead of a liability because she knew a thing or two about chemotherapy timelines and their effect on cure rates. In an e-mail to me, Mom said, "Brother, I hate this! I hate pulling strings. I just want to be me and have things happen the way they are supposed to. But when it is someone you love, sitting on your hands in hopes that it all falls into place is not an option."

During our time of dilemma, we, as always, received numerous e-mails of support and encouragement, urging us to take heart that everything would work out in the end. Many spoke of reminding themselves on days they felt overwhelmed and frustrated, that others have struggles that are much worse. I always appreciated these e-mails, however, I never wanted anyone to live their life by my reality. On the other hand, if it made them think in a more optimistic manner, I was all for that!

Other replies urged us to keep our sense of humor:

> The preacher's Sunday sermon was "forgive your enemies." He asked, "How many have forgiven their enemies?"
>
> About half held up their hands. So he repeated his question.
>
> Now about 80 percent held up their hands. He repeated his question again.
>
> All responded, except one elderly lady.
>
> "Mrs. Jones, are you not willing to forgive your enemies?" asked the preacher.
>
> "I don't have any," she replied.
>
> "Mrs. Jones, that is very unusual. How old are you?" asked the preacher.
>
> "Ninety-three," she replied.
>
> "Mrs. Jones, please come down in front and tell the congregation how a person who has lived such a long life cannot have an enemy in the world," instructed the preacher.
>
> The little sweetheart of a lady tottered down the aisle and said, "It's easy, I just outlived all those b—s."

> Our lives begin to end the day we become
> silent about things that matter.
> —Martin Luther King Jr.

November 4, 2003: Connections

Well, after a few days filled with angst, the ball is rolling. My dad will start a three-day course of chemo tomorrow, proceed with the GCSF next week, and move on to harvesting stem cells the week of November 17.

My mom is to credit for this sudden turn of events. Through her knowledge and connections, she appealed to the nurses and physicians involved in my dad's treatment. She assertively pointed out that the longer we wait on a brand-new remission, the greater chance we have of another relapse, or the inability to collect enough stem cells for transplant.

My mom feels horrible that she had to pull strings, and my dad feels a little like my mom should have just sat back and waited. But unfortunately, I don't have that much faith in our health-care system. We have wonderful physicians and fantastic nurses, but some things in our current health-care system are beyond their control. That said, I'm glad we don't live in the United States!

Nonetheless, we are filled with a million different emotions right now: relief, fear, sorrow, guilt . . . It is difficult to handle this roller coaster, but it's been a successful ride so far, and we have to continue to believe that this last stretch will be a successful one as well. I know that it won't be easy, but it's a necessary evil in order to beat this monster again. We will continue to be relieved and thankful that this show is on the road now. We will continue to let fear be a factor, but not a major one, because it's that fear that will keep us on top of things (as it has done this week), but we also recognize that fear can also cripple us. We will allow our sorrow to happen whenever it needs to; we don't need to be superheroes through all this, and we have a right to our emotions. I'm encouraging my mom to stomp all over any feelings of guilt she may have, because if it hadn't been for her, we would not be where we are today. The only shameful thing that could have happened this week is that she did not do anything with her knowledge and power. She must stand tall and proud because I believe she just saved her husband's life.

Thank you again for your thoughts and prayers. And most of all, thank you for allowing me the e-mail space to keep you informed. This is immensely therapeutic for me.

Karen

> Worry will not rob tomorrow of its sorrow,
> but it will sap the strength of today.
>
> —A. J. Cronin

November 15, 2003: Transplant Week No. 1

We successfully completed transplant week no. 1, and are into week no. 2. My dad spent last Thursday through Monday (November 6-10) at the Cross Cancer Institute receiving chemotherapy. Ran and I and our three kids left for Toronto on Friday, so we received updates by phone until we arrived home on Tuesday. My dad did very well through the weekend, but ended up putting on fourteen pounds of fluid due to the extra IV fluids he received to combat some potential side effects to his kidneys from one of the chemotherapy drugs. Once the chemo ended, he spent an extra day in hospital receiving drugs to get rid of all the fluid—he lost ten pounds in one day. How's that for a weight loss program! He's now at home, spending most of his time on his computer. He can't go out much because his white blood cell and platelet counts are so low that he's very susceptible to viruses and bacteria. When he does go out, he wears a mask; and when an outsider visits, they wear a mask too. In the middle of flu season, one can't be too careful! Fortunately, the blood transfusion he received before discharge has kept his hemoglobin up, so he's not as tired as he would have been otherwise.

My mom is doing okay . . . again, I'm more worried about her at this point than I am about my dad. I have every confidence that he will pull through this just fine. Things may get ugly, and it won't be easy watching him go through all that, but knowing that the result will be positive keeps my spirits up. But my mom knows too much. She waits through each twenty-four-hour period for a fever to develop, in which case, she needs to get my dad into hospital immediately. She worries about whether the chemo is administered in exactly the same way that she once did it and in the way that she taught her student nurses. She worries that the bone pain he's feeling from the GCSF is actually a tumor in his spine. Her friends and family are trying to take her mind off things by getting her out of the house for short stints. She's set up all her scrapbooking paraphernalia on her dining room table so that she can still be in the same house as my dad, but can transport herself back in time as she puts together new scrapbook pages.

The plan for week 2 includes a continuation of the GCSF drug that he took this week to increase his stem cell count in preparation for harvesting, as well as regular visits to the Cross to evaluate his blood counts. Week 3 will be the week of November 24 when he will visit Canadian Blood Services to have his stem cells harvested. This whole process is really rather amazing.

The fact that anyone figured out how to do all this, and even surmised that it might work, just blows my mind. My dad has something called a central line, or broviac catheter, which allows the medical staff to run more than one IV at a time, and it runs directly into an artery and into his heart. It also allows them to draw blood without poking him several times a day. How did someone even dream that one up? And when my dad receives his stem cells back, those cells will just know that they have to make their way from the vein that they're deposited into, all the way to my dad's bone marrow. Astounding.

All this has made me realize how important research and human trials are. Can you imagine how those folks who went ahead of my dad felt, being the guinea pigs? Not knowing whether the treatment would actually work, not knowing if they were getting a real drug or a placebo, not knowing if the treatment/drug would save them or kill them.

Right now, we're in the easy stages . . . come the first week of December, things may get dicey. That's when my dad will start the high-dose chemo to prepare him to receive his stem cells back again. But the plan is to have Christmas dinner at my house, with my dad in attendance! As an early birthday gift, we're giving him all the hardware and software he needs to webcam with his grandkids, since those little virus machines can't come anywhere near him right now. I hope all is well with all of you. Enjoy the time leading up to the holidays!

Karen

There are a few phrases stuck in my head that I heard Dad say many times. One of them is "Carry on." We tried our best to do just that. Randy and I were considering replacing the carpet in our home with hardwood, so I carried on by scheduling estimators to come to our house. A friend moved her home based business to a retail location, and I carried on by attending the grand opening. Mom carried on by having grandkids over for sleepovers and taking them to the Edmonton Symphony Orchestra's *Symphony for Kids*.

Sometimes, carrying on was easier said than done, but ultimately, it was healthy for all of us, including Dad. Preparation for transplant was a round-the-clock process. Nurses moving in and out of his room to hang blood, platelets, and medication resulted in a severe lack of sleep for Dad. This, in turn, caused him to be quite crabby! Carrying on with other things and not always being at the hospital allowed Mom, Barb, and I to avoid a tongue-lashing or two!

> What lies behind us and what lies before us are tiny matters,
> compared to what lies within us.
>
> —Walt Emerson

November 21, 2003: Transplant Week No. 2

Hello!

Transplant week no. 2 started off on a bad note, but is ending on an extremely sweet note.

Last Saturday night, my dad developed a fever, which meant he needed to go to emergency immediately. At that point, he had no white blood cells to speak of to fight any infection. Despite his best efforts to steer clear of bugs, he couldn't avoid them, because with no white blood cells, your own bugs begin attacking you. So my mom took him to emergency at the U of A where he spent the remainder of the night hooked up to the latest and greatest antibiotics, and waiting for an isolation bed at either the U of A or the Cross Cancer Institute. Since he had no white blood cells, the staff in emergency had to do blood cultures in order to determine the type of bug they were dealing with so they could treat it with the right antibiotics. Blood cultures take anywhere up to twenty-four hours, so it wasn't until late afternoon on Sunday when they figured out what they were actually dealing with. Both my sister and I had head colds, so neither one of us could help our parents out by being at the hospital. My mom spent the better part of 48+ hours with my dad as he was eventually transferred from emergency to a bed in Hematology at the U of A.

By Monday afternoon, my dad was transferred to the Cross, and his white blood count was at 100 (normal is anywhere between 5,000 and 10,000*). He was given another blood transfusion, as well as

---

* (2006) *White Blood Cell Count (WBC) and Differential.* Retrieved March, 2011 from http://www.rnceus.com/cbc/cbcwbc.html

platelets, plus antibiotics every two hours 'round the clock. Needless to say, he didn't get much sleep. On Tuesday, his white blood count was at 200—at this point, a 100 percent improvement is nothing to sneeze at! We were all excited. But that excitement didn't compare to the tremendous feelings we experienced as his counts jumped to 900 on Wednesday and 3,200 on Thursday! The minimum number of white blood cells required to start harvesting stem cells is 1,000, so he was able to start that process yesterday.

We felt a superb sense of relief that he was actually at Canadian Blood Services having his stem cells harvested, but at the same time, we were aware that they might not be able to collect enough stem cells, due to the cumulative amount of chemo he has had over the last eight years (in order to freeze and re-introduce the stem cells, they need to collect 3 million cells). But those fears were laid to rest last night when Canadian Blood Services reported that in three hours of harvesting they collected 2.8 million cells! So, presumably, another three-hour session today will give them more than enough to work with.

We are now looking forward to two weeks of smooth sailing during which my dad will have normal blood counts, and he will feel like his old self again. He hasn't seen his grandkids in weeks, and is very anxious to do so, before he gets back into hospital. We also purchased an early birthday present of webcam hardware and software, so we'll spend time getting that set up so he doesn't have to go through grandkid withdrawal again!

Karen

During his time off, Dad sent e-mails back and forth with a hematologist, a colleague and dear friend of Mom's. Being privy to the e-mails made me realize for the first time that the brave exterior Dad had was very much just an exterior—he was full of thought surrounding his treatment and more afraid than he let on. The engineer in him clung to numbers and statistics, and his e-mails were very concise, unemotional, and full of logic—also character traits of Dad! The hematologist used the same concise language, peppered with metaphors, in order to answer Dad's questions and put his mind at ease. He also suggested questions that Dad could ask of his physicians and was extraordinarily comforting. A true gem.

Another indicator of Dad's feelings were the e-mails he sent to his sister in Calgary. Dad wasn't always overt with his affection, especially with his sister and parents, but e-mails describing his treatment and trying to make it more understandable for them were his way of saying he cared about them. He used humor and spoke in positive terms:

> I know this won't be a day on the beach in Maui but I am quite positive it will work. They have done literally hundreds, perhaps thousands, of stem cell transplants at the Cross over the years and I cannot imagine there is anything for which they are not prepared. So for a couple of weeks I will probably wish I was somewhere, anywhere else, but after that things will begin to improve and by spring I should be in pretty good shape.

Perhaps not exactly what they needed or wanted, but in the end, it was his way of saying he loved them.

Success means having the courage, the determination,
and the will to become the person
you believe you are meant to be.

—George Sheehan

December 6, 2003: Genesis

Hello, all!

We are at the cusp of . . . well, a lot of things, I guess. We are at the cusp of the rest of my dad's life, of several weeks that will be full of sleepless nights, of a few weeks of antiemetics to treat the chemo side effects, of many years of worry that the cancer will return despite our best efforts; but most of all, we are at the cusp of a dream come true.

My dad will be admitted to the Cross on Monday, December 8, to begin the final stage of his stem cell transplant. On Tuesday, he will begin six days of high-dose chemo to kill off any last cancer cells in his body, and as a result, many other cells in his body. It will be extremely tough on him, and we expect severe side effects. On Monday the fifth, his own stem cells will migrate from an IV bag to his bones, where they will begin the task of rebuilding his bone marrow, and his life. It will be months before he has any amount of energy back, and years before he feels like himself again. We hope to have him home for the New Year, but celebrations will be quiet, I'm sure.

When I heard last week about the schedule in place for my dad, I was amazed by how I felt both a sense of relief and a sense of fear at exactly the same time. Relief that we are finally here, and that things are moving ahead without having to wait until the New Year (there was initial concern that nursing staff over the holidays would not be high enough to accommodate his transplant), and fear over what my dad has to endure over the next several weeks.

41

I have no doubt that the transplant will be successful, and that he will remain in remission. What I am most fearful of is seeing my dad in a way that I've never seen him before and not being able to help him. I am a helper and a fixer and not being able to make things right is a source of frustration for me. Aside from having cancer twice, my dad has always been strong and healthy. I always relied on him taking care of me. Now, the tables are turned. Even during his treatments, he was tired and without hair, but all that was bearable for me. But now, I am gearing myself up for things that I can only anticipate may happen. I anticipate that, over the next few weeks, I will watch him use every ounce of energy he has just to roll over in bed. I anticipate that I may have to put on my dental hat again and pull a few things out of my bag of tricks to help him clean his mouth when he has too many mouth sores to brush. I anticipate that I may have to hold a bowl for him while he vomits. I anticipate that I will watch him lose pound after pound and turn into a shadow of his former self. I anticipate that I will send many a leftover to my mom so that she will continue to eat during this ordeal. I anticipate that I will rely on my sister's composure and medical knowledge to keep me grounded. I anticipate that my dad will give us all a thumbs-up when he is ready to celebrate a late Christmas dinner (the Jasper Park Lodge has Christmas in November, so why can't we have Christmas in January?).

Having said all that, I'm working very hard at trying to stay focused on the destination and not the journey. After all, "worry will not rob tomorrow of its sorrow, but it will sap the strength of today" (unknown).

Karen

This was a very emotional time for all of us—as if it could get any more emotional! The sense of being on a roller-coaster hit again: great news because we were moving ahead in timely fashion, yet "Oh my goodness, how rough the next few weeks will be!" The news left Mom a bit speechless; her e-mail to friends and family simply read,

> Just heard from the transplant nurse that Don will be admitted Monday the eighth to start chemo on Tuesday and transplant on December 15.

My inbox was deluged with e-mails of support from near and far. Everyone was sick at the thought of what Dad would undergo over the following several weeks, but also very grateful that we had the opportunity to see him regain his health. Several people reminded us that we were all in their prayers, and although I am not a religious soul, it meant a lot to know that there were so many people sending us strength in one way or another. Many relayed stories of friends and family members who endured cancer treatments with outstanding success. At once, I felt comfort in those statistics, yet also found myself saying, "Yeah, but my dad's cancer is a relapse, and it's Hodgkin's, and he's almost sixty." If only someone could provide us with some kind of guarantee.

Certainly, by this point in the process, I was very thankful that I decided a few years earlier to be a stay-at-home mom for a time. Between my husband's travel for work, Dad's illness and raising three young kids, there weren't too many leftover hours in the day.

> Progress always involves risk. You can't steal
> second base and keep your foot on first.
> —Frederick B Wilcox

December 15, 2003: T = -1 and Counting

The medical staff at the Cross count like NASA during this whole transplant procedure. Last Tuesday, when chemo started, we were at day -7. Now, we're on day -1, and it's a day off chemo before tomorrow's stem cell transplant on day 0. The whole process is not unlike rocket science in that it is very technical, very black and white, and very calculated. Fortunately, we had some extremely competent and compassionate medical staff who brought a human component to the week.

The week had its ups and downs, but all in all, we're very thankful that all went as well as it did. Last Tuesday, my dad received an extremely high dose of a drug called Etopocide, which normally makes patients extremely sick. Apparently, the last fellow in for the same procedure started tossing his cookies as soon as the Etopocide hit his veins and didn't stop until after his transplant was done, despite all the antiemetic cocktails the doctors tried on him (including the medicinal Mary Jane!). He had to drink water just so there was something in his stomach to throw up. Fortunately, the Etopocide did not affect my dad that severely. He experienced a few chills on Tuesday, but was otherwise very chatty and in good humor. On Wednesday, when I visited, he seemed anxious that I leave so he could get back to work on his laptop! Thursday was a different story, however. His body finally reacted to the chemo, and he experienced extreme fatigue, a drop in blood pressure, nausea, vomiting, and diarrhea. His mind also started playing tricks on him, and he experienced a bit of psychosis and agitation. With no sleep, and chemotherapy constantly dripping into his veins, he felt so crappy by Friday that he requested no visitors except my mom. On Saturday he asked her to stay overnight . . . that's a big request coming from my dad, who, all along has said that hospital visiting hours are for the visitors instead of the patients, and nobody really needed to be with him at all!

My dad had an extremely knowledgeable nurse on Saturday who figured out that one of the antiemetic drugs (Decadron) was causing the agitation and psychosis. They have no choice but to give very high doses of Decadron and Zofran with this protocol, because the chemo is at such high doses, but instead of continuing the Decadron after the initial dose, they switched it to Gravol. That seemed to help my dad turn the corner and get his side effects under control.

Yesterday was day -2, and the last day of chemo, with a drug called Carmustine. We were told to expect the worst because Carmustine is "nasty." But it's almost as though my dad needs the nasty stuff to feel well! If he gets the chemo that's not so nasty, that's when his body gives in! By day's end, my dad was eating ice cream, going for walks, and very coherently chatting about the capture of Saddam Hussein. Imagine even caring about world events when you've been confined to a hospital room for a week and dealing with the side effects of poisons in your body! When I left last night, he was experiencing horrendous stomach cramps, but word this morning is that the codeine they gave him helped, he slept well last night, and he's looking forward to a day off today.

What I learned this week:
- Celebrate each small step in the journey. I was elated last night as I drove to the Cross to visit my dad because I realized that we made it through a week of high-dose chemo, relatively unscathed. What's more, we're at the end of the chemo altogether! We have some tough days ahead as my dad's blood counts drop, but that will give us another opportunity for celebration when they start rising. Imagine the party mood when he gets to go home from the hospital!
- Honesty. Everyone has their part to play in helping my dad recover. When my dad started vomiting, I realized that dealing with the pukes is not my forte, so being at the hospital at that time would not be helpful. My mom and sister (mostly my mom) took over hospital duty temporarily, and I helped in other ways: decorating my mom and dad's Christmas tree, sending leftovers to my mom, being an

end-of-day sounding board for my mom, and going shopping for special toothbrushes and toothpaste for my dad.

- One body can tolerate more than you might think. Thank goodness all my dad's organs are in good working condition. His heart won't give in to the toxins flowing through his body, and his liver and kidneys are working at full capacity ridding his body of the chemo, with no signs of throwing in the towel.

Chat with you in a week's time!

Karen

All in all, Dad did amazingly well through the first week of transplant chemo. The side effect that lingered for him was diarrhea, which caused his potassium and magnesium levels to drop. IV and oral doses of potassium as well as IV doses of magnesium brought the levels up, but maintenance of normal levels didn't succeed for quite some time.

The rest of the team (Mom, Barb, and I) also did amazingly well over the course of the week. Certainly, we were busy taking shifts at the hospital, and filling roles as needed, and being busy is physically exhausting. But what was more difficult was the emotional exhaustion. So many things were beyond our control, and we had no choice but to roll with things as they occurred. That is often easier said than done. All we could do was maintain our focus and courage as we watched a person we cared about a great deal suffer. Oh, and the other thing we could do was hold on to hope that the stem cell transplant would be successful, and Dad would be home soon.

Speaking of hope, one evening as I left his bedside, I said to Dad, "I hope that I have your genes so that if I ever end up with cancer, I'll be able to tolerate it as well as you do." To which he replied, "I hope you never get cancer." And then he winked at me. Another rare moment of observing the scared, vulnerable side of Dad.

Hope is an interesting thing. Religious or not, hope is something you can never allow yourself to let go of during a situation like this. Sometimes, the only thing that got us through the day was retreating to our own individual places of determined hopefulness.

Pain nourishes courage. You can't be brave if
you've only had wonderful things happen to you.
—Mary Tyler Moore

December 20, 2003

Hello, everyone!

I struggled to get started on this e-mail as well as the last, and at first, I wasn't sure why. It's not as though there isn't a lot to tell you about. For all the other e-mails, all I did was write what I felt, so what's the problem now?

After a lot of reflection, I realized that when my dad was diagnosed back in August, I had a pretty firm grip on my feelings because those feelings tended to last for a week or two. Now, things change from day to day, and my feelings change at the same pace. One day, my dad is upbeat, sitting up in bed, chatty, and energetic. And then, not twenty-four hours later, he's a completely different person; he's subdued, crabby, and wiped right out. So I find it difficult to grasp on to one theme or feeling to write about.

Nonetheless, here's what happened this week:

On Tuesday, as my aunt says, the fat lady sang, and she sang very well. Tuesday was transplant day, and all went off without a hitch. We were warned that there could be some major complications, and that we would be overcome by a horrible smell in my dad's room (due to the preservative used for the stem cells). None of the complications occurred, and his room simply smelled like creamed corn (not that I like creamed corn, but the smell was more than bearable!). So my dad enjoyed a day or two of relative calm, save for a few bouts of abdominal cramping, for which morphine did the trick.

Then Thursday happened. Right on schedule, my dad fell victim to the high-dose chemo. He developed mouth sores, which actually line his whole digestive tract (i.e., mouth, throat, esophagus, stomach, intestines, and colon). They are extremely painful at all times, but are especially painful when eating. He doesn't have an appetite to begin with, but he forces down a popsicle or two every day and tries other things like cold fruit and ice chips. The morphine dulls the pain enough so he can sleep. He's also still suffering from abdominal cramping and diarrhea. He's been running a fever for two days now, and that's because his own body's bugs are attacking him while he has no defenses to fight them off. And with no hemoglobin to speak of, he's just plain tired. All this is par for the course, and the medical staff anticipate that he will turn the corner in a week's time when his stem cells start to kick in.

Today, as I left the hospital, I heard a song on the PA system by John McDermott, one of my dad's favorite artists. Before I realized it, I was sobbing, and that shocked me. After all, I know my dad is going to recover, he's not going to die from this, and that everything he's experiencing is expected and treatable. The medical staff are wonderful and are keeping a close eye on him. I guess it's just difficult to watch a parent go through this. And being the control freak that I am, I find it frustrating that I can't do anything to fix this. All I can do is sit by his bedside and read a book and just be there if he needs me to fetch a popsicle, move his bedside table closer, adjust his blankets, and ask his nurse for more morphine.

But as my dad says: this too shall pass, and better days are ahead.

Merry Christmas and Happy Hannukah to you and your family!

Karen

The going was getting tough, so we all concentrated on being tough, moving forward, and being hopeful. The Christmas and Hannukah seasons overlapped in 2003, and since my husband's family is Jewish and mine is not, we busied ourselves with celebrating two Festivals of Light all at once. Dad would spend Christmas in the hospital, so we decorated his room with a miniature Christmas tree—one of those fiber optic jobs that change color and twinkle softly—as well as Christmas drawings created by the grandkids. The Christmas dinner that all patients received in the hospital was hysterical—two lonely rubbery pieces of unrealistic-looking turkey. It even brought a chuckle to Dad's belly and put a smile on his face. My kids had a visit with Dad on Christmas Eve, and Barb's kids went up to the hospital on Christmas morning. Dad took delivery of a few gifts at each visit, as well as a stocking from Santa, but I know he felt that the very best gifts he received were the visits from the grandkids.

Grandma P made the trek from Calgary to Edmonton for the Christmas holidays. With Barb and I taking shifts at the hospital, Mom was able to spend some time with Grandma P, which was good therapy for both of them. We left Dad to rest on Christmas Eve, and all congregated at Mom's house for dinner.

Christmas morning found us receiving the most wonderful gift of all: Dad's white blood cell count was 300! Now, a normal white blood cell count ranges from 4,500 to 10,000, so you may wonder what all the excitement was about. Well, on Christmas Eve, Dad's count was zero. An increase of any amount told us that the stem cell transplant worked, and his own body was beginning to make its own blood cells. We were far from being home-free, but it was an *immense* step in the right direction! To celebrate, I gave Dad a bright red T-shirt with They're Back! embroidered on the front.

Still recovering from the effects of the transplant chemo, Dad had an allergic reaction to the blood transfusions that he received. He developed a rash, rigors, fevers, and shortness of breath, resulting in a drop in the level of oxygen in his blood. His medical team changed the transfusions to irradiated single donor transfusions and put him on antihistamines and painkillers to help with the side effects of the allergic reaction. On the upside, in between the allergic reactions, Dad felt so much better than he did the week before. He did morning and afternoon laps (up to three!) around the hospital unit with his dancing partner (alias for IV pole) and sat up in a chair and visited for an hour or so at a time.

One quiet evening in Dad's hospital room, Mom and Dad chatted about traumatic events in people's lives. Dad commented on the human brain's ability to overcome such events and even forget how traumatic they were at the time. He likened it to women delivering babies and doing it again and again! Dad hardly remembered the horrible hours during the allergic reaction to the blood transfusions, and his brain was slowly forgetting the trying days of the pretransplant chemo–although his sore derriere was a reminder of the diarrhea induced by that chemo!

Looking back at this chapter's e-mail, I realize that when I spoke of hearing the John McDermott song and I said "He's not going to die from this," what I really meant (but would have denied then) was, "He may die from Hodgkin's, but he won't die from this particular treatment." There's that determined hopefulness I spoke of before.

How do you eat an elephant? One bite at a time.

—Unknown

January 9, 2004: Baby Steps

That's the only way I can think of to describe the last two weeks. These days, we don't see as many dramatic increases in how well my dad feels, but by the same token, we don't see him fall as hard either.

My dad was discharged last Monday (January 5), and is very happy to be home eating home cooked meals, and sleeping in his own bed. From December 31 to January 4, he was at the hospital during the day, but received night passes to sleep at home. As some of you may know, sleeping in a hospital isn't exactly easy, so those night passes were very precious! Now that he's discharged, he only has to be back at the Cross every couple of days for blood work, and at that time, they top him up with whatever he needs (whole blood, platelets, magnesium, potassium). So far, however, he hasn't needed any topping up. The nurses told him today that he's doing better than average at this point in time, so we're very pleased with that.

My dad has likened the effort that it takes him to walk to what he thinks it must be like for people climbing Mt Everest where oxygen is at a premium. Every step is an effort. In order to keep my dad moving while the weather is too cold to walk outdoors, (it's very tempting to sleep the day away when you are so tired and it's chilly outside), he rented a treadmill, and it's set up in the family room by the TV. He's slowly increasing the time he spends on the treadmill each day, while still having access to the Discovery Channel. My parents also moved their piano to my house to make room for a computer desk in an upstairs bedroom, requiring my dad to go upstairs each time he wants to work on his computer (which is several times a day!).

My mom and her menopause have to be extremely understanding, because my dad is feeling the cold temperatures more than the rest of us. In addition to wearing a sweater and a toque 24/7, he insists that the house be kept at twenty-four degrees! If my mom didn't deserve a medal before, she certainly does now!

Most days, my dad has a pretty decent appetite, but he still gets the odd wave of nausea. He's focusing on eating foods high in magnesium and potassium so that he can get rid of the liquid magnesium he has to take each day. But he discovered through an article in this week's Edmonton Examiner, that anything with calcium in it inhibits the absorption of magnesium. And many of the foods that contain magnesium also contain something else that inhibits the absorption of magnesium. Go figure! So, he and my mom put together a list of what drugs he takes when, and what foods he eats when, so as to ensure that he's getting the most of his medication and nutrition. It all gets very complicated!

Upward and onward. My mom and dad have booked an eighteen-day cruise from Vancouver through the Panama Canal to Ft Lauderdale. They leave September 29, and will spend a few days at the Kennedy Space Centre, and Epcot before heading home in late October. At first, they thought they'd go with a cheaper cabin on the ship, but then decided to go all out (well, not all out, because you can get a penthouse suite for $20,000 a person!), and get a verandah suite. Depending on which side of the ship they're on, they'll be able to watch sunrises or sunsets on their verandah. All the power to them!

So, slowly, but surely, we're winning this race. My dad was pretty teary the other day when he thanked me for all I did while he was in the hospital. He says that he's not sure what he would have done without his three ladies. I'm not sure what I would have done without the ability to chat through all this with all of you. So thank you very much for allowing me into your life on a weekly basis for the past several months.

Here's wishing you health and happiness in 2004 (and always)!

Karen

Determined hopefulness didn't always come easily. I recall a conversation with a dear friend during which I was quite doom and gloom where Dad was concerned. I was nervous on the eve of his first follow-up visit with the oncologist. Even though by New Year's Eve, Dad's chin was showing signs of peach fuzz, his recovery felt so slow to me. Plus, the liver involvement that was present way back in August was nagging at me—I wanted Dad's oncologist to tell me whether the cancer in his liver would factor into Dad's long-term recovery. Would that liver involvement rear its ugly head again at some point?

When each of my daughters turned four, I took them to Maui to visit Mom and Dad as they vacationed there for two months. Jake's turn was to come when he turned six—I wanted to *know* that Dad would be able to share Maui with his grandson, just as he did with his granddaughters.

I closed that conversation by admitting defeat, if only for a moment, to determined hopefulness. I actually said to my friend, "I know we must carry on as though he has another twenty or thirty years with us, but I think deep down I know that this disease will one day claim my dad."

> Keep on going and the chances are you will stumble on
> something, perhaps when you are least expecting it. I have
> never heard of anyone stumbling on something sitting down.
> —Charles F Kettering

January 31, 2004: My Dad's First Follow-Up Appointment

Hello! Just thought I'd spread the encouraging news about my dad's health. He had his first follow-up appointment with his oncologist yesterday, and all is going well. We compared the CT scan report from August (enlarged lymph nodes all over the place, enlarged liver, enlarged spleen, lesions on the liver . . . basically a page and a half of doom and gloom) to the CT scan report from last week, which was two lines long: lymph nodes are normal size, liver is normal size, spleen is normal size, lesions on the liver are gone! His magnesium levels are still not where they should be, so he will continue the magnesium supplements. His white blood count and hemoglobin levels are almost at normal, so they will continue to monitor his blood work on a weekly basis. So despite the fact that my dad is still walking with a cane, and he tires very easily, he is doing well. We went seed shopping the other day, even though it was -40 degrees Celsius with the windchill, and I'll be helping him seed plants for the remainder of the winter and into the spring. Jake had a sleepover last night. Plans are all in place for the cruise that my parents will embark on in the fall, and they are in the process of booking two months in Maui for this time next year (Jake's turn!). The next followup with his physician is in a month's time. I hope to be able to report the same, or better, good news then!

Karen

The month of February saw Mom make a trip to Calgary to visit Grandma P, as well as Dad's sister and Mom. She also finalized plans to attend the 2004 Canadian Curling Brier in Saskatoon, Saskatchewan with a dear childhood friend.

Dad's recovery continued to be excruciatingly slow and, at least to me, tenuous. Perhaps it was because when he was in treatment, even though it wasn't a barrel full of laughs, I felt as though something was being done; we were actively accomplishing something. By this point, we were back to the waiting game where treatment was over, and we just had to wait and see how things turned out. I enjoyed talking to Dad on the phone more than I enjoyed seeing him because his voice sounded just like it used to, and in my mind, I could picture him the way he used to look, with a full head of hair and a belly ballooned by a semi-daily dose of scotch.

A long-term side effect of the chemo cropped up with a fair degree of intensity during this time. Peripheral neuropathy, or damaged nerves in the extremities, was something Dad experienced during the chemo he went through eight years earlier, and it prevented him from playing his guitar. It also made his fingers and toes very sensitive to cold, so being outside for any length of time in Canada's winter weather was painful for him. The case he developed after the transplant was much worse. His feet were extremely painful, whether he was standing on them, and the pain kept him up a lot at night. Medication helped only minutely.

Some days, however, were better than others. One day I'd find him tired and lackluster, and the next I'd discover that he was over at a friend's house fiddling around with electronics. The good days were not to last, unfortunately.

By the beginning of March, Dad developed a cold that settled in his chest. He moved to the spare bedroom on the main floor of the house, partly so he wouldn't have to use so much of his limited energy to get to his comfy chair in the family room, and partly so he wouldn't keep Mom awake all night with the coughing. I'm not sure the latter actually mattered because Mom used one of our old baby monitors to keep an ear on Dad 'round the clock. Mom kept offering nutrition of some sort, and every so often, Dad would agree to juice or a bowl of broth and noodles.

With no relief in sight, Dad was admitted to the Cross because he was having trouble breathing. An initial diagnosis of pneumonia was treated with antibiotics and oxygen. Feeling in familiar territory, Barb and I urged Mom to carry on with attending the Brier in Saskatoon. She agreed, after leaving us a list of phone numbers and instructions. Mom was giving Dad injections of a drug called Eprex, which stimulated production of red blood cells in Dad's bone marrow. Barb, also a nurse, received a rundown from Mom about when the injections needed to be given (Monday and Wednesday), where to find the Eprex syringes (in the butter keeper in the fridge), and how to transport the Eprex doses safely between home and hospital (insulated lunch bag with a cold pack). Mom also made Barb and I commit to keeping her apprised of Dad's every move, and writing down every number that was spoken by a medical professional so we could give her a detailed play-by-play every time she called. Agreements in place, Mom hopped in her car and headed to Saskatoon.

Mom contacted Dad by phone every day at about supper time between curling draws. Barb and I took turns calling Grandma P in Calgary, and I continued e-mail updates to my aunt. After speaking with Mom on the phone in Dad's hospital room one evening, Dad commented that we must hold on to the lists of numbers that we were tabulating, as Mom would surely want to scrapbook them. Dad never lost his sense of humor.

Days passed with doctors, nurses, me, Barb, Mom and even Dad tossing out possibilities to explain the setback. Dad had a fever and, virtually, no appetite to speak of. Antibiotics were changed because the initial drug didn't appear to be making any inroads. Then the theory changed to the possibility that the pneumonia was viral, in which case no amount of antibiotic would do a thing. Dad insisted that the cause of his fever was not Hodgkin's because the fevers were different than the ones he had before he was diagnosed. Dad wasn't worried, but he was discouraged. I was too, given that I had to help him put his socks on, and after changing for bed, he had to have a rest before he could sit up and take his medication.

After a while, Barb and I could no longer hide our anxiety from Mom, and she returned from Saskatoon before the Brier ended. While she drove, Barb and I were at Dad's side as he underwent a CT scan. A bronchoscopy was also scheduled, with the intent of removing crud from the bottom of Dad's lungs, culturing it, and ultimately determining what drug to treat the crud with. After the CT was completed, however, someone realized that the contrast dye used in the CT scan would cause some sort of interference in the bronchoscopy procedure, so the bronchoscopy was delayed by a day.

The upside of the delay was that Mom arrived home in time for Dad's transfer to the University of Alberta hospital and to be nearby while Dad had the bronchoscopy. The procedure itself went well, and the surgeon told us that although there was some muck in Dad's lungs, there was also a lot of healthy tissue, and no sign of tumors. We glommed onto those bits of good news like they might just blow away in a mild spring breeze. The end result of the CT and the bronchoscopy was a change in diagnosis from bacterial or viral pneumonia to pneumosystis—a fungal pneumonia common in people with compromised immune systems. Treatable, but time was of the essence.

Test results from the bronchoscopy were expected to take a couple of days, so in the meantime, Dad's physician started him on IV antifungal drugs. These drugs can have potentially severe side effects, so Dad was premedicated with painkillers and antihistamines. After a successful few hours with no sign of trouble, Barb and I decided to attend an out-of-town scrapbooking retreat that would see us gone for three days, but with twenty-four-hour cell phone communication.

Three days turned into one for Barb and a few hours for me, as we received increasingly frequent phone calls from Mom that were filled with angst. Leaving my car behind in rural Alberta, Barb and I inched our way back into Edmonton on icy, snowy roads. Luggage that wouldn't be too damaged by the falling wet snow was in the open bed of Barb's truck, and delicate scrapbooks and supplies were piled on the seat between us and on my lap. As we drove, we attempted small talk and tried to keep things light and optimistic, even though our insides were full of the angst we inherited from Mom's final phone call. Back at the hospital, Dad's physicians decided to perform a lung biopsy, since the bronchoscopy results were inconclusive. Barb and I arrived late in the evening, just in time to have some one-on-one, heart-to-heart time with Dad before he went into surgery.

Mom, Barb, and I waited anxiously outside the intensive care unit where we knew Dad would end up after surgery. As soon as we saw his gurney being wheeled down the hall toward the unit, the three of us raced to Dad's side and chauffeured him into ICU. The ICU nurses and doctors got him settled, and as they performed a bedside dance that seemed all too familiar to them, I asked Dad if he was doing okay. He nodded yes and squeezed my hand. I gave him a kiss on the forehead and said good night.

Not wanting my young kids to ask questions about why I was home so soon from scrapbooking, I spent the night at Mom's. I felt huge pangs of regret about not asking Dad if he wanted someone to stay the night with him. If I were in his shoes, I'd be scared and would want the comfort of family close by. Mom and Barb reassured me that the medical staff would not let anyone stay the night—they needed their space to get Dad's care sorted out. But to this day, I wish I would have at least asked.

To keep our faces toward change and behave like
free spirits in the presence of fate is strength undefeatable.
—Helen Keller

March 14, 2004: We're Back in Hospital Mode Again

Hi, all!

Just a note to let you know that my dad is very sick again. Two weeks ago, he came down with a cold, which quickly moved into his lungs. On Thursday March 4, he was admitted to the Cross Cancer Institute because he was having trouble breathing. They thought it was pneumonia, so started treating him with antibiotics and felt that everything would be better by the time the weekend was over. He continued to get worse and worse, requiring more and more oxygen to breathe, so they transferred him over to the U of A Hospital on Friday, thinking that he'd be close to ICU if he needed it over the weekend. By day's end on Friday, they decided to do a lung biopsy, since the bronchoscopy they did earlier in the week didn't show what type of infection he has. He had the biopsy yesterday evening and is now in ICU on a respirator. He has made some progress today and is conscious. He communicates with us by hand motions and writing on a piece of paper—the respirator prevents him from talking. He's got more IVs than I can count, but with one-on-one nursing care, he's well taken care of. The nurses and physicians in the ICU are exceptional, both with my dad and with my mom, sister and me.

We're all very frustrated because he was recovering nicely from his stem cell transplant. He is, as always, the eternal optimist and is viewing this as a setback in his recovery, but believes that he will come through this just fine. The rest of us believe that most of the time, but we do have our moments of sheer panic.

We're told that they will let the respirator do the work of breathing for him for the next couple of days. This is to allow his lungs to rest, since they've been working so hard for so long. Keep your fingers crossed that by week's end, my dad will be out of ICU and back on to a regular unit.

Karen

Dad's oxygen requirements continued to increase, and his ICU nurses regularly suctioned out his lungs because he was retaining fluid in them. Dad's nurses also told us that he was "fighting" the respirator and not allowing it to do the work on behalf of his lungs, so his doctors decided to sedate him. The plan was to keep him unconscious until his lungs began to heal and his oxygen requirements lessened. Steroids were added to the cocktail of drugs Dad was receiving by IV, with the intent of reducing inflammation in his lungs.

The two pieces of good news available to us were as follows:

1. Dad asked via pen and paper when he would be able to eat and drink–a sign that he was getting better and his appetite was returning.
2. The lady across the hall was in exactly the same position as Dad–Hodgkin's, stem cell transplant, lung problems–and was packing up to go home that very day.

An alternate explanation for number one above was that his brain was not receiving enough oxygen, so his thought process wasn't 100 percent. I chose to ignore Barb when she told me that the recovery rate in PICU where she worked was 80 percent, as opposed to 50 percent in adult ICU.

It's the possibility that when you're dead
you might still go on hurting that bothers me.
—Keri Hulme

March 15, 2004: 9:34 PM

Hello, all,

Unfortunately, I have some terribly tragic news to share with you tonight. My dad passed away this afternoon, shortly after four o' clock. When I arrived at the hospital this morning, I found that he had deteriorated somewhat overnight, however, everyone was still hopeful that things would turn around. As we waited patiently for the results of the biopsy, things continued to get worse. The doctors and nurses were just not able to keep him oxygenated well enough to keep him alive. I have some wonderful friends who took care of my kids for me, and I raced to the hospital to be with my dad. When I arrived, he was in cardiac arrest. They were able to revive him, but not for long.

I am in a complete state of shock. This has all happened so fast, and I'm angry that it happened at all because he was recovering from the transplant so nicely. Understandably, my kids have also taken the news hard. They developed such a close relationship with both of my parents, and my kids were the light of my dad's life. I imagine my dad is also in shock because he never believed this would happen. Even late this morning, when the doctors told us that they would put my dad to sleep to allow the ventilator to do the work for him, he said he wasn't scared. I believe that he always believed he would get through this.

I will keep you posted of the funeral arrangements. It may be a few days away because an autopsy will be done to try to get more information about what exactly it was that caused all the problems.

Karen

It's funny the things you remember so very clearly. I sat on my family room couch that afternoon and put my head back for a short rest before heading out to pick Rachel up from school. Sarah and Jake kept each other occupied in the nearby playroom, giggling as they played some imaginary game. Friends agreed to care for all three kids that evening so I could go to the hospital to see Dad (Randy planned on being out with clients that night), so this was my last chance to put my feet up before heading into a busy evening.

As I took a deep, relaxing breath, the phone rang. It was Mom calling from the hospital to tell me that Dad was not doing well, and his physicians suggested that all family members be at the hospital. Flashes of scenes from the TV show *ER* went through my mind as I thought, *This is what the doctors on TV say when someone is dying*. With much haste, I gathered Sarah and Jake together and took flight to Rachel's school, frantically hoping to meet sooner rather than later with the friends who were to care for my kids that evening. As I encountered them, I thrust child car seats at them, and burst into tears, explaining between sobs that I had to flee to the hospital to be with Dad.

My heart was in my throat out of fear for Dad's life rather than fear for my own as I raced as fast as my minivan would go toward the University Hospital. When Barb asked me later how I got to the hospital so quickly, I replied that any NASCAR driver would be proud. Clinging to determined hopefulness, I couldn't let go of the possibility that Dad would rally; however, I also did not want to be absent from his side, just in case he didn't make it.

Traffic parted like the Red Sea, and a parking space nearby the hospital entrance magically appeared as I drove by. Pretending to be Paula Radcliffe, I took off running at a determined and panicked clip. Halfway between my van and ICU, with my lungs screaming for air, I came to the realization that I was nowhere near Paula's league when it came to running. I stopped long enough to allow the heart seizing feeling in my chest to subside and then carried on at a rookie jogger's pace.

Mom and Barb met me at the ICU entrance, and Dad's physician followed shortly after. Dr. M ushered the three of us into one of the meeting rooms on the unit–I know now that being ushered into a meeting room is a sure sign that things aren't going to turn out well. Mom and Barb knew this immediately, but at the time, I remained blissfully ignorant. As we sat at the meeting table like we were in some corporate office downtown, Dr. M explained everything the medical team attempted for Dad that day. Heroic efforts were made, but they just couldn't keep Dad on the good side of the 50 percent adult ICU success rate.

Of course, I received many, many caring and thoughtful replies to my grief-stricken e-mail advising of Dad's death. Nothing anyone said could change what was, but it meant so much to hear from those who e-mailed, called, dropped off meals, sent cards, and made donations in Dad's memory. Statements such as, "I cried a thousand tears for you," and "With heavy hearts," and "It seems so unfair," and "Please consider yourself hugged . . . hard" resonated with me.

An e-mail from one of my childhood friends was particularly meaningful for me, and motivated me to focus on the good memories that Dad left behind, not only for my sake, but also for the sake of my children.

> I cannot begin to tell you how moved I have been by your loving correspondence about your father, and how deeply saddened I am to hear that he succumbed to his illness. There is literally nothing adequate I could say to you at a time like this, but I must say something. I know your loss must be profound, the pain so deep it is impossible to express.

> I really feel for you. And I too feel the loss of your father—he was such a good man and his passing has taken me back down memory lane to our childhood of best-friendship—the neighborhood, the community, the relationships with one another and with one another's parents. The playing they did with us, the driving, the indulgence, the favors, the trips here and there, the zoo, the game farm, Mulhurst, the jokes. I find myself thinking of him in gratitude for the many sacrifices of time and energy he made for us. To pitch a tent for us to sleep in the yard in, to build a balance beam for hours and hours of fun. And how we took it for granted at the time, eh. Yes, it is so hard to believe all that the passing of time brings, the many blessings and the intense struggles. I have never been very religious, but

at a time like this, I simply cannot believe that Don is really gone. Surely he is still with us, not only in our hearts, minds, souls, but most of all in spirit. Perhaps—I hope—he is in a better place. Free, free of illness and encumbrances, the struggle his life had become. I know he will be sorely missed, and in the meantime, I can't help but to hold out hope that eventually we will all encounter one another again . . . that maybe, just maybe, it really isn't over at all. Please accept my heartfelt condolences, know that I can only imagine the pain of this loss for you and for your family, especially your children. Also please pass along my condolences to your mother and Barb. And please know what fond memories I have of your father. He touched so many lives, including my own.

—NP

Papa, can you hear me?
—Barbra Streisand as Yentl

March 17, 2004: Arrangements

Hi, everyone,

We finalized the arrangements for the celebration of my dad's life. He did not want a service of any sort, so we decided to have a reception in his memory. It will take place from 5:00-9:00 PM on Saturday, March 20, at Hainstock's Funeral Home, 9810 34 Avenue, Edmonton. Casual attire, please. Please feel free to pass this information along to whomever you feel may be interested—all are welcome, including kids!

An obituary will begin running in tomorrow's *Edmonton Journal* and *Calgary Herald*.

I change how I feel from minute to minute—this is so much harder than I ever expected. I keep thinking about how fast time went from my childhood to now!

There is a tradition in the Jewish community of planting trees in Israel for any kind of life event. Today, I received in the mail a note from Rachel's teacher, saying that she has paid for a tree to be planted in Dad's memory in Israel. I was, once again, brought to tears. Not only by her thoughtfulness but also because it made me feel that my dad's spirit will live on not only in the plants that we plant this summer but also way across the world in a land where a group of people he held close to his heart live and celebrate life.

I've always known of this tradition, but didn't really think about it all that much. Now I feel the impact of how meaningful it is. I continue to be awestruck by the thoughtfulness and compassion of those around us.

Karen

A bit of a flight of thoughts, which tells you how scattered I felt at the time.

The day after Dad died, the kids stayed home from school, and we met at Mom's house to plan Dad's funeral. Mom's best friend, who became a widow about seventeen years earlier, also spent the day with us. She is like family to us, and her presence there was so very comforting. We talked about what Dad wanted in his service and how to write the obituary. I had two requests for the obituary. One was that we begin it by saying "It is with great sorrow that we announce the death of Don" rather than "It is with great sadness." The word *sorrow* seemed to more accurately reflect the depth of our feelings than the word *sadness*. The second was that we specifically name all the members of his family, including his parents, sister, niece, and nephew. It was my small way of attempting to mend some fences.

A few days before Dad's funeral, Mom, Barb, and I met at the funeral home to view Dad's body before he was cremated (Dad chose cremation because he didn't want to take up too much room in the earth). My kids were so young, so I didn't take them with me, and although viewings are not typically my cup of tea, I was not about to miss out on the last opportunity I had to say good-bye to Dad. I hoped it would take away the sick feeling that I had that Dad still did not understand why he wasn't waking up from the sleep that the doctors in ICU induced. And as strange as it sounds, I wanted to apologize for not brushing his teeth for him while he was intubated in ICU. I don't know if it was even possible to do, but if it was, maybe I could have made Dad more comfortable.

Surprisingly, the viewing was not as unpleasant as I thought it would be. The funeral home dressed Dad in some clothes that Mom gave them, and although Dad looked more like a wax figure from Madame Tussauds, it was good to see him and talk to him one last time. I specifically remember his nose being very bony, and commented to Mom and Barb that it reinforced how much weight Dad lost over the previous seven months.

Dad was not religious, and did not like to be the center of attention; so instead of a formal service, we planned a reception that reflected Dad's wishes and his personality, and where people could gather to remember Dad. Several tables around the room held displays that told a story of Dad. One table had a flat of seedlings at varying stages of growth to show Dad's love of gardening, another a scrapbook of photos from Maui to show Dad's love of Maui, another table showcased a collection of Dad's beloved electronics projects, another table had numerous bottles of scotch of varying quality as well as plastic shot glasses so people could share in Dad's love of scotch by partaking in a "wee dram." The family table showcased Dad's love of family, with crafty creations made by the grandkids, as well as photos and other memorabilia. My brother-in-law also put together a slide show of photos set to music from the CDs that we made for Dad. I tried a bit of scotch in Dad's memory, but immediately apologized to him: "Sorry, Dad, there are many things I will do to keep your memory, but drinking scotch is not one of them!" The slide show was especially meaningful for me because it helped me begin to erase some of the not-so-pleasant memories of late and replace them with good old memories.

I was amazed and touched by how many people showed up at Dad's reception. Everyone from our family dentist and physician to people Dad worked with many years prior at Alberta Transportation. Every so often, someone would walk through the door and I would collapse sobbing, grateful for their thoughtfulness and compassion.

The only downside (other than the obvious!) of Dad's reception was that Grandma McT decided not to attend. She felt the trip from Calgary would be too difficult and worried that getting to the upstairs room where we held the reception wouldn't be possible due to her limited mobility. While the trip may not have been easy for her, I was disappointed that, after all the difficulty Dad faced with determination and courage, she couldn't take a lesson from him and travel to Edmonton to say good-bye to her son. The funeral home had elevators to take her from the main floor to the second floor, and I think the reception would have helped her cope a little too. It took awhile for me to be comfortable with not being able to own Grandma McT's choices and to listen to another piece of Dad's advice that rang in my ears: "Get on with the show."

It only hurts when I breathe.

—Shania Twain

May 4, 2004: Diagnosis

Hello, everyone,

We have what is a tentative diagnosis on the cause of death for my dad. It seems that it wasn't pneumonia at all, but most likely drug toxicity due to all the chemotherapy that he had over the years, for which there is no treatment and, thus, no cure. One doctor was leaning toward a possible fungal infection, caused by an extremely rare fungus; however, our infectious disease specialist friend assures us that the amount of fungus found in my dad's lungs was in amounts neither great enough nor concentrated enough to cause death. It's so unfortunate that the very treatment that was supposed to cure my dad ended up killing him. However, my dad's hope for the future was to do whatever was necessary to improve his chances of survival. He was given a 51 percent chance of survival with chemo and a stem cell transplant, and my dad didn't live life as though he was on the wrong side of those odds.

We are still awaiting my dad's autopsy results, and we expect that we will be well into the winter months before we receive those. Probably November or December. The diagnosis we have today could change with those results, but for the moment, this is what we're going with. In a way, it's a little easier to cope with a diagnosis that we know was untreatable.

We are all doing well. Thankful that my dad died in the spring and not the fall. He loved the spring and summer months, and grieving is much more bearable when it can be done in the sunshine with the birds singing rather than in minus twenty in the dark. My mom and

I have successfully grown a good portion of the seeds that my dad and I had planned on planting together . . . my dad would be proud of us!

We're also thankful for the safe and healthy arrival of my sister's second baby. He is a week and a half old now and is a content and happy baby. His middle name is the same as my dad's middle name, and he certainly has my dad's quiet, introspective disposition (so far!). Makes one ponder the continuity of life!

My kids continue to talk about Grandpa. Jake is having the most difficulty "getting it." Each time we go to my mom and dad's house, Jake takes a wander around the house looking for Grandpa. Sarah talks the most about the memories she has, and Rachel is the most likely to end up in tears over Grandpa. Rachel turns eight this Saturday, and it will be bitter sweet because I can still see my dad holding his first grandchild for the first time.

I hope all is well with you! Happy spring!

Karen

If Tomorrow Starts Without Me . . .

If tomorrow starts without me,
And I'm not there to see,
If the sun should rise and find your eyes
All filled with tears for me;
I wish so much you wouldn't cry
The way you did today,
While thinking of the many things,
We didn't get to say.

I know how much you love me,
As much as I love you,
And each time that you think of me,
I know you'll miss me too;

So when tomorrow starts without me,
Don't think we're far apart,
For every time you think of me,
I'm right here, in your heart.

–Unknown

So, it's been seven years. My eldest is getting ready to graduate from grade 9, and my twins will finish their first year of Junior High. Rachel and Sarah speak fondly of Dad, remembering all of the good things about Grandpa and the time they shared with him. Jake still dissolves into tears without notice, typically at bedtime, as he remembers Dad, and still questions why he can't share a life with Grandpa. He cuddles with his 'Grandpa Bear' for comfort. All three of my kids are growing and maturing into people I believe Dad would be proud of.

We received Dad's autopsy results in May, 2004. The medical examiner stated Dad's cause of death as Acute Respiratory Distress Syndrome (ARDS) that resulted in respiratory failure, most likely caused by a bit of a vicious circle. That is, Dad received a drug as part of his chemo regimen for which treatment with supplemental oxygen is not recommended as it causes lung tissue to increase in density. However, when Dad came down with the cold at the beginning of March he needed supplemental oxygen as he was having trouble breathing. But, the more oxygen he was given, the denser his lungs became, which, in turn increased his supplemental oxygen requirements, and so on, and so on . . .

Two pieces of information stood out when we read the autopsy report. The first was that Dad had an 80% blockage in one of the arteries in his heart, and 70% blockage in another. He was a bit of a sitting duck for a heart attack. The most significant piece of information, however, was that the medical examiner detected residual or recurrent Hodgkin's disease in some of Dad's lymph nodes. What this means, ultimately, is that even if Dad did not fall prey to ARDS, he wouldn't be with us today because all of the stops had already been pulled out to treat Dad's Hodgkin's relapse, and it didn't work.

There isn't a day that goes by that I don't think of Dad. When I have a question that needs answering, I find myself thinking, "Dad will know the answer to that . . . oh . . . crap." And, every time Rachel sings, my heart swells with pride, yet breaks with sorrow, wishing Dad could personally witness his granddaughter and the vocal talent she inherited from him. I continue to be surprised by the emotions this writing brought forth. Dad and I often did not see eye-to-eye, however, I loved him and respected him, and wish he were still here. But, not at all costs.